MW00974089

~ Many thanks to my parents, Mr. &
Mrs. D. J. Murray, my sister Susan
Murray, and Peggy and Angelo
SanFratello for support ~

~ Credit and thanks to Ed Bullinger
for Bebe's front cover photo and
image editing throughout the book ~

BeBe . . . Meet the Yorkie Pup

by
Libby Murray

Dedicated to everyone

who loves Yorkshire terriers.

The search had been a long one

To find just the perfect pup.

Finally, I found her ~ I knew it
When she looked up.

She turned around, brightly smiled,

And did a dance of glee.

This tiny Yorkshire terrier

Had captivated me!

BeBe settled into her new home ~

In her eyes, a touch of fear.

She looked around and wondered

If she was going to like it here.

BeBe was small in the soft, round bed

That was her very own.

Sometimes she'd take a nap there;

It would fit her when she's grown.

BeBe was into everything ~

Just like an active pup!

She was even running all around

With her nose stuck inside

a Styrofoam cup!

BeBe's first big challenge
Was to climb up on the bed.

She kept on jumping up and down ~

You could only see her bobbing head!

After several days of trying,

She finally made it up.

So, curled into the comforter
Was where you'd find the sleepy pup!

When you talk to BeBe,

She'll try hard to understand.

She'll look at you, cock her head,

As if to say, "May I hear that again?"

BeBe's learned a lot of words,

And if one starts with PET ~

She looks as though she's asking,
"Where are we going, and are we
there yet?"

The sound of thunder, or just the word,

Makes BeBe hide her head.

She'll take off at lightning speed ~

Then, lie trembling beneath the bed.

She's got those pointed Yorkie ears

That move in all directions.

Watch her ears, and you will see ~

She's reading your expressions!

Whenever there is something

BeBe can't quite figure out,

She'll stick her small, pink tongue out,

And then look all about!

BeBe's full of wit and wonder,

And displays it every day.

She shows it in her attitude and

In the way she loves to play.

When she's playing chase or catch

With a favorite worn-out ball,

She's agile as a kitty cat,

And never takes a fall.

BeBe loves her Teddy bears ~

Her quacking duck and all.

But in her mind, there's nothing like

That fast and spinning, white golf ball!

BeBe can smell the golf ball;

She can hear the golf club's whack.

She'll chase a golf ball anywhere,

And always bring it back!

Since she cannot use a golf club,

She'll use her tongue or nose.

You'd think she's playing soccer ~

   It's the challenge, I suppose.

Chasing after golf balls

Has put BeBe in a very tight place.

It's almost like she sets it up ~

Another challenge for her to face!

BeBe likes her special friend ~

His name is Sidney Cat.

Sometimes they rub noses;

Then, Sidney's had enough of that!

BeBe likes to entertain you;

She likes to flirt and tease.

She jumps and runs and dodges;

The little Yorkie loves to please.

It's delightful dressing BeBe up

In her sweaters of green and blue.

She acts as though she doesn't mind;

BeBe likes playing dress-up, too.

BeBe spreads her love around
To each and everyone.

She knows just how to interest you,

And let you share the fun!

You may have heard that pups can smile,

And this should prove it's true.

She sees a camera, strikes a pose,

And then, she smiles for you!

To see and play with BeBe,

Friends will travel far.

BeBe is a Yorkie charmer,

And she knows that she's a star!

She's BeBe . . .

funny,

little,

Yorkie

pup!

~ The End ~

You are about to meet a very captivating Yorkshire terrier. You'll get to know BeBe as she grows from a tiny, fuzzy pup to a five- year- old complete with the Yorkie's long, shiny coat.

Discover BeBe's one special interest, and find out if she is anything like your pup.
Is BeBe a diva or a darling?

Welcome to BeBe's world . . .

As an elementary school teacher, now retired, Ms Murray found the perfect inspiration in BeBe to continue her interest in children's books. Ms Murray, a native of NC and a UNC-Chapel Hill graduate, completed her teaching career in Cobb County in Metro Atlanta. She now resides in Jupiter, FL.

3505871

Made in the USA